THE MASTERY OF RELAXATION TECHNIQUES

CALM YOUR MIND, CLEAR MENTAL CLUTTER, IMPROVE MIND-BODY CONNECTION, AND ACHIEVE TOTAL CLARITY AND INNER PEACE

FREDDY JOY

ABOUT THE AUTHOR

Freddy Joy, Author of "The Mastery of Relaxation Techniques."

F reddy Joy never set out to become a writer. Her journey began with a simple yet profound desire—to share her experiences and insights on managing stress and boosting productivity to lead a fulfilling life. Armed with a strong academic foundation, she holds a Master's degree in Psychology (MSc) from Dr. B.R. Ambedkar Open University, specializing in practical applications of research in human behavior and psychology. Additionally, she earned a "Certificate in Community Health" from Indira Gandhi National Open University, equipping her with knowledge to address key issues in public health.

Freddy lives in Guntur, Andhra Pradesh, India, where she balances her professional pursuits with her most cherished role as a mother of two. Whenever she can, she devotes her time to her children, finding joy and inspiration in their presence. Her writing is a testament to her passion for helping others navigate life's challenges and unlock their true potential.

CONTENTS

THE POWER OF RELAXATION FOR A BALANCED LIFE

"Almost everything will work again if you unplug it for a few minutes, including you."
— *Anne Lamott*

Introduction: Why Relaxation is a Skill, Not Just a Luxury

In today's fast-paced world, relaxation often takes a backseat to productivity, deadlines, and responsibilities. Many people treat relaxation as an indulgence—something to be earned after a hard day's work. However, science and experience tell a different story: relaxation is not a luxury; it is a fundamental skill essential for overall well-being.

Consider the story of Sarah, a high-achieving marketing executive who prided herself on being "always on." She thrived on back-to-back meetings, late-night emails, and constant notifications. Over time, stress took a toll on her health—she suffered from chronic headaches, insomnia, and a weakened immune system. It wasn't until Sarah was diagnosed with severe burnout that she realized the importance of structured relaxation. By incorporating daily mindfulness practices and breathing exercises, she reclaimed her energy, creativity, and mental clarity. Her transformation wasn't accidental; it was the result of intentionally developing the skill of relaxation.

Sarah's story is not unique. The ability to relax effectively can transform physical health, mental clarity, and emotional resilience. This chapter will explore the science behind relaxation, its impact on the brain and body, and how mastering this skill can help us navigate the stress epidemic of modern life.

The Science Behind Relaxation: How It Affects the Brain and Body

1. The Nervous System and the Relaxation Response

The human body operates through two main nervous system states: the sympathetic (fight-or-flight) and the parasympathetic (rest-and-digest) systems. When stress dominates, the body remains in a heightened state of arousal, leading to increased cortisol levels, high blood pressure, and mental fatigue. However, activating the parasympathetic system through relaxation techniques lowers cortisol, slows the heart rate, and promotes healing (McEwen, 2007).

2. Brainwave Shifts and Cognitive Benefits

Research in neuroscience has shown that deep relaxation shifts brainwave patterns from high-beta (associated with active thinking and stress) to alpha and theta waves, which are linked to creativity, problem-solving, and deep relaxation (Tang et al., 2007). Meditation, yoga, and deep breathing exercises have all been found to enhance cognitive function, memory, and emotional regulation.

3. Relaxation and Physical Health

Studies have demonstrated that individuals who regularly practice relaxation techniques experience lower rates of cardiovascular disease, better immune function, and improved digestion (Benson et al., 2011). Relaxation is not just about feeling good—it actively prevents long-term health complications caused by chronic stress.

Overcoming the Modern-Day Stress Epidemic

The Digital Overload Problem

In an era where digital notifications, emails, and social media dominate daily life, relaxation has become harder to achieve. The constant barrage of information keeps our nervous system in a perpetual state of alertness. Emerging research suggests that digital minimalism—reducing screen time, turning off unnecessary notifications, and engaging in offline activities—can significantly lower stress levels (Newport, 2019).

Work-from-Home Burnout

The shift to remote work has blurred the boundaries between professional and personal life, making it difficult to truly unwind. A study by Microsoft (2021) found that remote workers experienced a significant increase in work-related stress due to longer screen time and lack of physical separation from workspaces. Strategies such as scheduled breaks, mindful transitions between tasks, and structured relaxation can counteract this burnout.

Real-Life Story: John's Breakthrough with Relaxation Practices

John, a software engineer, struggled with anxiety and difficulty focusing. Despite being highly skilled, his productivity was declining due to constant mental clutter. After attending a mindfulness workshop, John implemented a simple 10-minute daily meditation practice. Within weeks, he noticed improved concentration, better sleep, and a greater sense of control over his emotions. His story highlights the importance of small but consistent relaxation habits in managing modern stress.

How This Book Will Transform Your Life

This book is designed to help you master the art of relaxation, not just as a temporary escape but as a lifelong skill. You will learn:

- **Practical techniques** to switch off stress and enter a relaxed state anytime, anywhere.

- **Scientific insights** into how relaxation enhances mental clarity, emotional stability, and physical health.

- **Actionable strategies** for integrating relaxation into daily life, even in high-pressure environments.

- **Interactive tools** like habit trackers and guided exercises to personalize your relaxation journey.

By the end of this book, relaxation will no longer feel like an elusive luxury—it will become a natural, essential part of your daily routine, leading to greater productivity, better relationships, and a more fulfilling life.

CHAPTER 1

UNDERSTANDING STRESS AND ITS IMPACT ON YOUR WELL-BEING

"It's not stress that kills us, it is our reaction to it." — Hans Selye

Introduction: The Hidden Costs of Chronic Stress

S tress is often perceived as a normal part of life, but chronic stress can take a toll on mental, emotional, and physical well-being. While short bursts of stress can enhance focus and performance, prolonged exposure to stress hormones can lead to anxiety, depression, and even physical illnesses. Understanding how stress operates and its long-term consequences is the first step toward building resilience and reclaiming control over our well-being.

Take the case of Laura, a high-performing executive who thrived under pressure—until she didn't. After years of continuous deadlines and neglected self-care, she found herself dealing with migraines, fatigue, and irritability. It wasn't until her doctor warned her about the dangers of chronic stress that she took action. Through targeted relaxation strategies, she reversed many of the negative effects and regained balance in her life. Laura's story is a testament to the power of awareness and intervention in managing stress effectively.

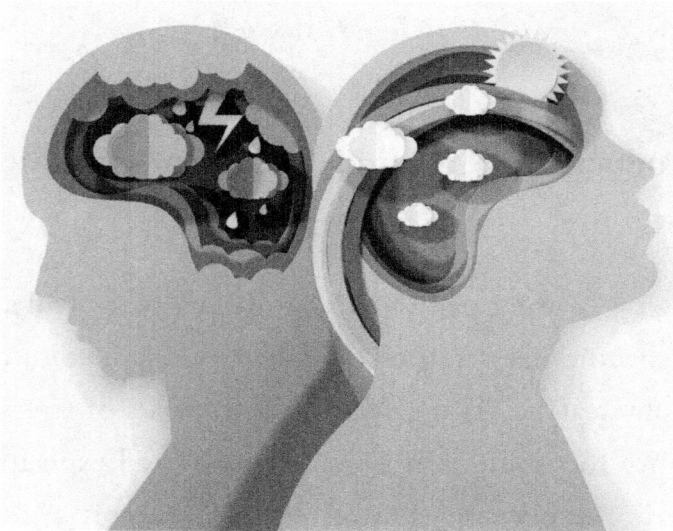

The Fight-or-Flight Response vs. the Relaxation Response

1. The Science Behind Stress and Its Effects on the Body

When faced with a perceived threat, the body's sympathetic nervous system activates the fight-or-flight response. This evolutionary mechanism prepares the body for action by increasing heart rate, raising blood pressure, and releasing adrenaline. While useful in life-threatening situations, chronic activation of this response can lead to serious health issues such as cardiovascular disease, insomnia, and weakened immunity (McEwen, 2007).

2. The Power of the Relaxation Response

Harvard researcher Dr. Herbert Benson introduced the concept of the relaxation response—a physiological state that counters stress by lowering heart rate, reducing blood pressure, and promoting a sense of calm (Benson & Proctor, 2011). Techniques such as meditation, controlled breathing, and mindfulness can activate this response, mitigating the harmful effects of chronic stress.

Identifying Stress Triggers in Your Daily Life

Common Sources of Stress

Understanding what triggers stress is essential for managing it effectively. Some of the most common stressors include:

- **Workplace Pressure**: Tight deadlines, job insecurity, and high expectations

- **Financial Concerns**: Debt, unexpected expenses, and job instability

- **Relationships**: Conflicts, social expectations, and emotional labor

- **Digital Overload**: Constant notifications, excessive screen time, and social media comparisons

Real-Life Story: Mark's Journey to Stress Awareness

Mark, a software engineer, found himself constantly overwhelmed. He was always checking emails, working late hours, and struggling to balance his personal life. After experiencing severe anxiety, he started tracking his stress levels and identified specific triggers—excessive multitasking and lack of boundaries between work and personal time. By setting clear limits and practicing digital detox, he regained focus and reduced stress significantly.

The Path to a Relaxed and Resilient Mindset

1. Developing Stress Awareness

Self-awareness is key to managing stress effectively. Keeping a stress journal, reflecting on daily emotions, and recognizing patterns can help individuals pinpoint their biggest stressors.

2. Practical Strategies for Stress Reduction

- **Mindfulness Meditation**: Studies show that regular meditation reduces cortisol levels and enhances emotional regulation (Tang et al., 2007).

- **Breathing Techniques**: Deep breathing exercises, such as the 4-7-8 technique, activate the parasympathetic nervous system, promoting relaxation.

- **Physical Movement**: Exercise releases endorphins, which improve mood and counteract the effects of stress.

- **Digital Detox**: Limiting screen time and creating tech-free zones can significantly reduce mental fatigue and overstimulation.

3. Actionable Takeaways

- Identify your top three daily stress triggers and develop a strategy to manage each one.

- Practice deep breathing exercises for five minutes daily.

- Set a 'stress-free' zone in your home where relaxation is prioritized.

Conclusion: Reclaiming Control Over Stress

Chronic stress does not have to dictate our lives. By understanding its impact, recognizing triggers, and implementing proven relaxation strategies, we can cultivate resilience and maintain mental and physical well-being. The key is consistency—small, intentional actions every day can create a profound shift in our overall stress levels.

CHAPTER 2

THE ART OF
DEEP BREATHING FOR
INSTANT CALM

"Feelings come and go like clouds in a windy sky. Conscious breathing is my anchor." —
Thich Nhat Hanh

Introduction: Why Breathwork is the Ultimate Stress-Buster

Breathing is an automatic function, but how we breathe can determine our stress levels, mental clarity, and overall well-being. Deep breathing techniques, rooted in ancient practices and supported by modern science, can activate the body's relaxation response, lowering cortisol levels and improving focus. Mastering breathwork is one of the simplest and most effective tools for achieving instant calm and long-term stress resilience.

Consider Lisa, a corporate executive who struggled with anxiety before big presentations. By practicing controlled breathing techniques daily, she transformed her ability to manage stress, improving both her performance and overall well-being. Her experience highlights the power of conscious breathwork in navigating high-pressure situations.

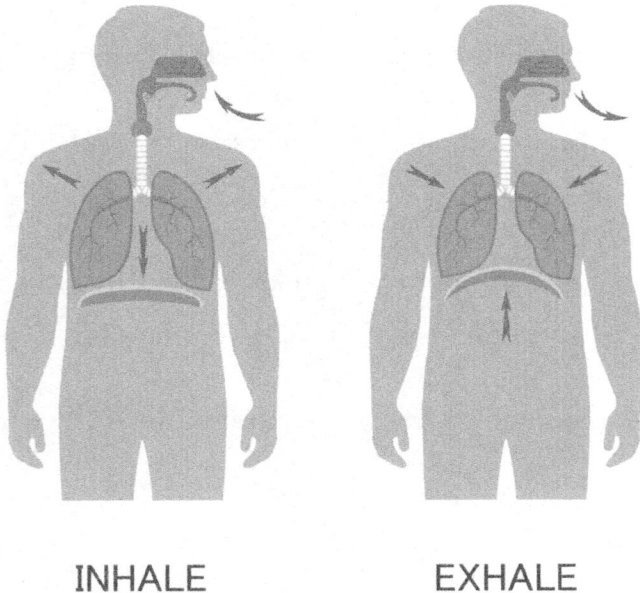

INHALE   EXHALE

Proven Breathing Techniques for Deep Relaxation

Diaphragmatic Breathing

Also known as belly breathing, diaphragmatic breathing encourages full oxygen exchange, slowing the heartbeat and stabilizing blood pressure.

How to Practice:

1. Sit or lie down in a comfortable position.

2. Place one hand on your chest and the other on your abdomen.

3. Inhale deeply through your nose, allowing your diaphragm to expand while keeping your chest still.

4. Exhale slowly through your mouth.

5. Repeat for 5-10 minutes.

Box Breathing

This technique is commonly used by athletes and military personnel to enhance focus and reduce stress.

How to Practice:

1. Inhale deeply through the nose for a count of four.

2. Hold your breath for a count of four.

3. Exhale slowly through the mouth for a count of four.

4. Hold the empty breath for a count of four.

5. Repeat for several minutes.

4-7-8 Relaxation Method

Developed by Dr. Andrew Weil, this method promotes relaxation and aids in sleep improvement.

How to Practice:

1. Inhale deeply through the nose for a count of four.

2. Hold the breath for a count of seven.

3. Exhale completely through the mouth for a count of eight.

4. Repeat the cycle four times.

Alternate Nostril Breathing (Nadi Shodhana)

A yogic practice that balances the nervous system and enhances mental clarity.

How to Practice:

1. Sit in a comfortable position.

2. Use your thumb to close your right nostril and inhale through the left nostril.

3. Close your left nostril with your ring finger and exhale through the right nostril.

4. Inhale through the right nostril, then switch nostrils again.

5. Repeat for 5-10 cycles.

How to Integrate Breathing Exercises Into Your Daily Routine

- **Morning Mindfulness:** Start your day with five minutes of diaphragmatic breathing.

- **Midday Reset:** Use box breathing during work breaks to refocus and recharge.

- **Stressful Moments:** Practice the 4-7-8 method before high-pressure situations.

- **Evening Relaxation:** Wind down before bed with alternate nostril breathing for deep relaxation.

Conclusion: Breathe Your Way to a Calmer Life

Deep breathing is a powerful yet accessible tool for managing stress and enhancing well-being. By integrating these techniques into daily life, you can cultivate a sense of calm, clarity, and resilience. The key is consistency—just a few minutes a day can lead to profound benefits over time.

CHAPTER 3

MASTERING MINDFULNESS AND MEDITATION FOR LASTING PEACE

"You should sit in meditation for twenty minutes every day—unless you are too busy. Then you should sit for an hour." — Zen Proverb

Introduction: The Power of Mindfulness in a Chaotic World

I n today's fast-paced world, the mind rarely gets a chance to rest. From constant notifications to looming deadlines, our attention is pulled in countless directions. This state of perpetual busyness contributes to heightened stress, anxiety, and even chronic health conditions. But what if there was a way to slow down, regain control, and cultivate a sense of inner peace? Mindfulness and meditation offer exactly that.

Scientific studies confirm that mindfulness and meditation significantly reduce stress and improve overall well-being. A landmark study conducted by Dr. Jon Kabat-Zinn at the University of Massachusetts Medical School found that participants in an eight-week mindfulness-based stress reduction (MBSR) program experienced substantial decreases in anxiety and an improved ability to handle stressful situations (Kabat-Zinn, 1990). With growing research backing their benefits, mindfulness and meditation have transitioned from spiritual practices to widely accepted wellness tools.

This chapter explores how mindfulness reduces stress, introduces practical meditation techniques, and provides actionable strategies to integrate these practices into daily life. Through real-life stories and scientific insights, you will discover how to harness mindfulness for lasting peace.

The Connection Between Mindfulness and Stress Reduction

Mindfulness is the practice of maintaining a moment-by-moment awareness of thoughts, feelings, bodily sensations, and the surrounding environment without judgment. Dr. Daniel Goleman, author of *Emotional Intelligence*, explains that mindfulness enhances emotional regulation, leading to improved mental clarity and resilience (Goleman, 2013).

The Science Behind Mindfulness and Stress Reduction

Research has shown that mindfulness influences the brain's structure and function. A study using MRI scans conducted by Harvard neuroscientist Dr. Sara Lazar found that regular mindfulness meditation increases gray matter density in the prefrontal cortex (responsible for decision-making and emotional regulation) while reducing activity in the amygdala, the brain's fear center (Lazar et al., 2005). These changes explain why mindfulness practitioners report lower stress levels and enhanced emotional stability.

Real-life Example: *John's Transformation* John, a high-level executive, was constantly overwhelmed with work-related stress. After attending a mindfulness retreat, he committed to a 10-minute daily meditation practice. Within months, he noticed improved focus, fewer emotional outbursts, and a greater sense of control over his reactions. His team even remarked on his newfound calmness during high-pressure situations.

Simple Yet Powerful Meditation Techniques

Practicing meditation doesn't require hours of commitment or an isolated retreat. The following techniques offer powerful benefits with minimal time investment.

Guided Visualization

Guided visualization involves imagining a peaceful scene or situation, helping the mind focus and reduce anxiety. Research published in *The Journal of Behavioral Medicine* suggests that visualization can lower stress hormones and enhance relaxation (Kwekkeboom, 2003).

How to Practice:

1. Find a quiet space and close your eyes.

2. Imagine yourself in a serene location, such as a beach or forest.

3. Engage all senses—hear the waves, feel the breeze, and smell the fresh air.

4. Spend 5–10 minutes immersed in this mental retreat.

Loving-Kindness Meditation (Metta)

Loving-kindness meditation involves cultivating feelings of compassion towards oneself and others. A study from Stanford University found that even a short session of Metta meditation increases feelings of social connectedness and reduces stress (Hutcherson et al., 2008).

How to Practice:

1. Sit comfortably and take a few deep breaths.

2. Silently repeat phrases like, "May I be happy, may I be healthy, may I be at peace."

3. Extend these wishes to loved ones, acquaintances, and even those with whom you have conflicts.

Body Scan Relaxation

This practice involves directing attention to different parts of the body, systematically releasing tension. Research in *Psychosomatic Medicine* indicates that body scan meditation enhances relaxation and reduces stress-related symptoms (Carlson & Garland, 2005).

How to Practice:

1. Lie down or sit comfortably.

2. Close your eyes and bring awareness to your toes, releasing any tension.

3. Gradually move upward, scanning and relaxing each body part.

4. Conclude by taking deep breaths and appreciating the relaxation.

Zen and Transcendental Meditation

Zen meditation focuses on seated breathing, promoting deep awareness. Transcendental meditation (TM) involves silently repeating a mantra to enter a state of restful alertness. A study published in *JAMA Internal Medicine* found that TM significantly reduces blood pressure and stress (Oman et al., 2008).

How to Practice:

1. Sit in a comfortable position with a straight spine.

2. Focus on your breath (Zen) or repeat a simple mantra (TM).

3. If the mind wanders, gently bring attention back.

4. Start with 10-minute sessions, gradually increasing over time.

How to Build a Daily Meditation Practice for Lifelong Relaxation

Consistency is key to experiencing the full benefits of mindfulness and meditation. Here are some strategies to integrate these practices into daily life:

Start Small and Build Gradually

Begin with just 5 minutes per day and gradually increase your meditation time as it becomes a habit.

Set a Dedicated Space

Create a calming environment for meditation, free from distractions. This could be a corner of a room with a cushion or chair.

Use Technology Wisely

Apps like Headspace and Calm offer guided meditations, making practice easier and more structured.

Pair Meditation with Existing Habits

Link meditation to an established routine—such as practicing before morning coffee or after brushing your teeth—to reinforce consistency.

Real-life Example: *Emma's Journey to Mindful Living*

Emma, a mother of two and a full-time remote worker, struggled with balancing her responsibilities. After committing to a daily body scan meditation before bed, she noticed improved sleep quality and reduced irritability. Over time, mindfulness became her go-to stress management tool.

Conclusion: The Lasting Benefits of Mindfulness and Meditation

Mindfulness and meditation are powerful tools for navigating life's challenges with greater ease. By cultivating present-moment awareness and integrating meditation practices into daily life, you can significantly reduce stress and achieve lasting peace. Whether through guided visualization, loving-kindness meditation, or body scans, there is a technique for everyone. The key is to start small, remain consistent, and gradually build a practice that supports lifelong relaxation.

—◦❖◦—

CHAPTER 4

UNLOCKING THE POWER OF PROGRESSIVE MUSCLE RELAXATION (PMR)

Introduction

Progressive Muscle Relaxation (PMR) is a powerful technique designed to alleviate stress, reduce anxiety, and enhance overall well-being. By systematically tensing and relaxing muscle groups, PMR fosters deep relaxation and a heightened awareness of bodily tension. In our fast-paced, high-stress world, learning how to harness the power of PMR can be transformative. This chapter explores the science behind PMR, its benefits, and practical steps to integrate it into daily life.

Progressive Muscle Relaxation

EDITABLE STROKE

Key Insights: Understanding PMR and Its Impact

What is PMR, and How Does It Work?

PMR, developed by Dr. Edmund Jacobson in the early 20th century, is based on the principle that muscle tension is a physical manifestation of stress. By engaging in a cycle of tension and release, individuals can train their bodies to recognize and counteract stress responses. Scientific studies have shown that PMR effectively lowers cortisol levels, reduces symptoms of anxiety disorders, and improves overall mental health (Jacobson, 1938; Bernstein & Borkovec, 1973).

A Step-by-Step Guide to Full-Body Relaxation

To practice PMR effectively, follow this structured approach:

1. **Find a Quiet Space** – Sit or lie down in a comfortable position.

2. **Breathe Deeply** – Inhale through your nose, hold for a few seconds, and exhale slowly.

3. **Begin Muscle Tension and Release** – Start from your toes and work your way up:

   ○ Tense each muscle group for about 5–10 seconds.

   ○ Release and feel the difference between tension and relaxation.

4. **Continue Through the Body** – Progressively move from the feet to the calves, thighs, abdomen, arms, shoulders, and finally the neck and face.

5. **Reflect on the Sensation** – After completing the cycle, take a moment to notice the relaxation and any

lingering tension.

How PMR Helps Improve Sleep and Reduce Anxiety

Research highlights PMR's efficacy in improving sleep quality and reducing insomnia symptoms (Mellman et al., 1995). The method activates the parasympathetic nervous system, which counteracts the body's fight-or-flight response. PMR is also effective in managing anxiety disorders and is frequently recommended in cognitive-behavioral therapy (CBT) programs (Conrad & Roth, 2007).

Real-Life Story 1: Overcoming Insomnia with PMR

John, a 45-year-old executive, struggled with chronic insomnia due to work-related stress. After implementing a nightly PMR routine, he experienced significant improvements in sleep duration and quality. Within weeks, he reported feeling more rested and focused during the day.

Pairing PMR with Breathing and Meditation for Maximum Impact

Combining PMR with deep breathing and mindfulness meditation amplifies its effectiveness. Techniques like diaphragmatic breathing and guided meditation enhance relaxation responses and provide a holistic approach to stress management.

Real-Life Story 2: Managing Anxiety Through PMR and Meditation

Emma, a college student, faced severe anxiety before exams. By pairing PMR with guided meditation, she reduced her panic episodes and improved concentration. Her case illustrates the synergy between relaxation techniques in managing psychological stress.

Conclusion

PMR is a scientifically backed relaxation technique with profound benefits for mental and physical well-being. By incorporating it into daily routines and combining it with

THE MASTERY OF RELAXATION TECHNIQUES

breathing exercises and meditation, individuals can achieve sustainable stress relief and better sleep quality.

CHAPTER 5

THE HEALING EFFECTS OF SOUND, MUSIC, AND NATURE THERAPY

"Music can change the world because it can change people." – Bono

Introduction

Have you ever noticed how a particular song can instantly lift your mood or how the sound of ocean waves can lull you into a state of deep relaxation? Sound has a profound effect on human emotions, cognition, and well-being. Across cultures and centuries, music, chanting, and nature sounds have been used to heal, calm, and energize. In today's fast-paced world, where stress is an inevitable part of life, leveraging sound and music therapy can offer an accessible and effective way to restore balance.

This chapter explores the science behind sound healing, the therapeutic effects of binaural beats and Solfeggio frequencies, and the benefits of immersing oneself in nature's symphony. We'll also provide actionable steps to create your personalized relaxation soundscape for maximum benefits.

Nature Sound Therapy

How Sound Frequencies Influence Relaxation and Healing

Sound therapy is not a modern invention. Ancient civilizations, from the Greeks to the Hindus, used specific frequencies for healing purposes. The Greek philosopher

Pythagoras believed that music had the power to heal both the body and the soul, a principle that continues to find support in contemporary research.

Scientific studies indicate that different frequencies affect brain wave activity, guiding the mind into states of relaxation, focus, or alertness. For example, delta waves (0.5–4 Hz) are associated with deep sleep and healing, while alpha waves (8–14 Hz) promote relaxation and mental clarity. A 2017 study published in *Frontiers in Psychology* found that exposure to relaxing music significantly reduced cortisol levels, the hormone responsible for stress (Chanda & Levitin, 2017).

Real-Life Story: The Music That Helped a War Veteran Heal

David, a former U.S. Army soldier, struggled with PTSD after returning from deployment. Traditional therapy provided some relief, but he found solace in an unexpected source—music. Through music therapy sessions that incorporated binaural beats and guided relaxation, he began experiencing fewer flashbacks and improved sleep. His therapist used specific sound frequencies to rewire his stress response, ultimately helping him reclaim his life.

Binaural Beats and Solfeggio Frequencies for Stress Relief

What Are Binaural Beats?

Binaural beats involve playing two slightly different frequencies in each ear, creating an auditory illusion that induces a specific brainwave state. Research has shown that listening to binaural beats in the theta range (4–7 Hz) can enhance deep relaxation and meditation (Gao et al., 2014). These beats are now used in sleep therapy, focus enhancement, and anxiety reduction programs.

The Power of Solfeggio Frequencies

Solfeggio frequencies are a set of tones that date back to ancient Gregorian chants. Each frequency is believed to have unique healing properties:

- **396 Hz** – Releases fear and guilt

- **528 Hz** – Promotes DNA repair and healing

- **639 Hz** – Enhances relationships and emotional balance

- **741 Hz** – Detoxifies the body and mind

- **852 Hz** – Boosts spiritual connection and intuition

A study published in *The Journal of Alternative and Complementary Medicine* (2018) found that listening to 528 Hz significantly reduced stress and promoted relaxation (Yamamoto & Shinagawa, 2018).

The Therapeutic Benefits of Nature Sounds and Forest Bathing

Why Nature Sounds Soothe the Mind

Natural sounds, such as rain, birdsong, and ocean waves, have a profound calming effect. According to research from *Scientific Reports* (2017), exposure to nature sounds shifts brain activity away from stress-related patterns and enhances the parasympathetic nervous system, responsible for relaxation (Lopez et al., 2017).

The Practice of Forest Bathing (Shinrin-Yoku)

Forest bathing, or Shinrin-Yoku, is a Japanese practice that involves immersing oneself in a natural environment to enhance well-being. Studies show that spending time in nature lowers cortisol levels, improves mood, and strengthens the immune system. A 2019 study from *Environmental Health and Preventive Medicine* revealed that just 20 minutes of nature exposure can reduce stress and increase a sense of calm (Hansen et al., 2019).

Real-Life Story: From Burnout to Balance

Samantha, a high-achieving executive, suffered from chronic burnout. She turned to forest bathing as a last resort after traditional stress management techniques failed. By integrating weekly nature retreats with calming soundscapes, she not only regained mental clarity but also significantly improved her sleep and emotional resilience. Her experience highlights the profound impact of reconnecting with nature's healing frequencies.

Crafting Your Personalized Relaxation Soundscape

To maximize the benefits of sound and music therapy, consider creating a personalized relaxation soundscape tailored to your needs.

Step-by-Step Guide:

1. **Identify Your Preferred Sounds** – Experiment with different genres of music, binaural beats, and nature sounds.

2. **Use High-Quality Audio** – Invest in good headphones or speakers for immersive listening.

3. **Integrate Sound into Daily Routines** – Play relaxing music while working, meditating, or before bedtime.

4. **Explore Sound Apps and Platforms** – Apps like Calm, Brain.fm, and Insight Timer offer guided sound therapy.

5. **Combine with Other Relaxation Techniques** – Pair sound therapy with breathing exercises, yoga, or progressive muscle relaxation for enhanced benefits.

Conclusion

Sound, music, and nature therapy provide a powerful, science-backed approach to stress reduction and emotional healing. Whether through binaural beats, ancient Solfeggio frequencies, or the soothing embrace of nature sounds, integrating these practices into daily life can lead to profound improvements in mental and physical well-being. By crafting a personalized relaxation soundscape, you can harness the power of sound to restore balance, enhance resilience, and cultivate lasting inner peace.

CHAPTER 6

MOVEMENT-BASED RELAXATION: YOGA, TAI CHI, AND STRETCHING

"Almost everything will work again if you unplug it for a few minutes, including you." – Anne Lamott

Introduction

Stress has become an inevitable part of modern life, affecting our mental clarity, emotional stability, and physical well-being. While many turn to medication or therapy for relief, an often overlooked but incredibly effective method lies in movement-based relaxation. Practices like yoga, Tai Chi, and stretching offer a natural way to reset the nervous system, bringing deep relaxation and renewed energy.

This chapter explores the mind-body connection in relaxation and provides practical techniques to incorporate movement-based practices into your daily routine. Through compelling real-life stories and scientific research, we'll uncover how these ancient techniques can foster resilience, mental clarity, and holistic well-being.

The Mind-Body Connection in Relaxation

The human body holds stress in physical ways—tight shoulders, clenched jaws, and stiff muscles. Movement-based relaxation addresses this by integrating breath, mindfulness, and physical motion to release stored tension. Studies have shown that practices such as yoga and Tai Chi reduce cortisol levels (Pascoe & Bauer, 2015) and activate the parasympathetic nervous system, promoting relaxation and emotional balance.

Real-Life Story: Sarah's Journey from Burnout to Balance

Sarah, a high-achieving marketing executive, found herself overwhelmed with chronic stress and anxiety. Despite trying therapy and meditation, she struggled to calm her racing thoughts. After joining a local yoga class, she noticed an immediate shift. The deep breathing and mindful movement helped her reconnect with her body, while the stretching released years of tension. Within months, Sarah experienced fewer anxiety episodes and improved her sleep, reinforcing the power of movement-based relaxation.

Best Yoga Poses for Stress Relief and Deep Relaxation

Yoga is one of the most accessible movement-based relaxation techniques, blending breath control, meditation, and physical postures. Some of the best yoga poses for stress relief include:

1. Child's Pose (Balasana): A grounding pose that stretches the back and calms the nervous system.

2. Legs-Up-The-Wall Pose (Viparita Karani): Reduces

swelling, improves circulation, and promotes deep relaxation.

3. Cat-Cow Pose (Marjaryasana-Bitilasana): Gently stretches the spine, releasing tension from the back and shoulders.

4. Corpse Pose (Savasana): Encourages total relaxation, integrating breath awareness and mindfulness.

Scientific research confirms yoga's effectiveness in stress reduction. A study published in the Journal of Clinical Psychology found that regular yoga practice significantly lowered anxiety and depression levels (Smith et al., 2017). The combination of controlled breathing, mindful movement, and meditation makes yoga a powerful stress-relief tool.

The Gentle Power of Tai Chi and Qigong for Inner Peace

Tai Chi and Qigong, often referred to as "meditation in motion," emphasize slow, controlled movements synchronized with deep breathing. These practices originated in ancient China and have been linked to improved mental clarity, reduced stress, and enhanced balance.

The Science Behind Tai Chi's Relaxation Benefits

A study published in Harvard Health found that Tai Chi reduces stress by lowering blood pressure, improving heart rate variability, and enhancing emotional resilience (Wayne et al., 2014). The fluid motions create a meditative state, shifting focus from stressors to present-moment awareness.

Real-Life Story: How Tai Chi Transformed James' Health

James, a 62-year-old retired teacher, struggled with hypertension and chronic fatigue. His doctor suggested stress management techniques, and James discovered Tai Chi at a local community center. Within weeks, he noticed reduced anxiety, improved mobility, and better sleep. Over time, his blood pressure normalized, and he felt a renewed sense of vitality. James' experience highlights the profound impact of mindful movement on both physical and mental health.

Stretching Routines to Release Tension and Restore Energy

Stretching is a simple yet effective way to alleviate stress by increasing flexibility, improving circulation, and releasing tight muscles. Here are some essential stretching exercises for relaxation:

1. Neck Stretches: Gently tilting the head side to side to relieve tension in the shoulders and neck.

2. Forward Bend (Uttanasana): Stretches the hamstrings and encourages relaxation.

3. Seated Spinal Twist: Enhances spinal mobility and relieves lower back tension.

4. Butterfly Stretch: Opens up the hips, an area where stress is often stored.

According to a study published in The Journal of Physical Therapy Science, daily stretching significantly reduces muscle stiffness and lowers stress-related cortisol levels (Sharma et al., 2018). By incorporating these simple movements, anyone can experience the benefits of relaxation through movement.

Pairing Movement-Based Practices for Maximum Impact

For optimal results, combining yoga, Tai Chi, and stretching with other relaxation techniques enhances their effectiveness. Pairing them with:

- Breathing exercises like diaphragmatic breathing increases relaxation.

- Meditation enhances mindfulness and focus.

- Music or nature sounds deepens the calming effect.

Conclusion

Movement-based relaxation is a powerful, accessible tool to combat stress and improve overall well-being. Yoga, Tai Chi, and stretching each offer unique benefits, from deep relaxation to enhanced mobility and mental clarity. By integrating these practices into your routine, you can cultivate a resilient, calm, and energized mind-body connection.

CONCLUSION: INTEGRATING RELAXATION INTO YOUR LIFESTYLE FOR LIFELONG BENEFITS

"Relaxation is the key to unlocking both productivity and peace of mind. When you allow yourself the space to recharge, you open the door to all kinds of possibilities."

Introduction: The Power of Relaxation in a Busy World

In today's fast-paced world, relaxation often takes a backseat. With constant demands on our time—from work pressures and family obligations to the omnipresent pull of digital notifications—many of us find ourselves running on empty. But what if we told you that relaxation isn't just about taking a break? What if it could serve as a foundation for better health, stronger relationships, and more focused productivity?

Understanding the importance of relaxation and incorporating it into your daily routine is more crucial than ever. Stress is a silent epidemic, impacting physical health, emotional well-being, and even the quality of our interactions with others. However, by actively prioritizing relaxation and cultivating a ritual that supports mental and physical calm, you can experience profound, long-term benefits.

In this chapter, we will explore the science of relaxation, why it's necessary for a balanced life, and how to integrate effective relaxation practices into your routine. We'll also look at emerging trends such as digital minimalism and how to overcome barriers to relaxation in today's busy world. Through real-life examples and actionable advice, we'll equip you with the tools to craft a personalized relaxation strategy that can transform your life.

Key Insights: The Science of Relaxation and Habit Formation

1. Understanding Relaxation and its Impact on Health

When we hear the word "relaxation," many people envision simply lying on the couch or taking a nap. While these are valuable forms of rest, true relaxation goes beyond passive downtime. It's about achieving a mental and physical state of calm and stillness that allows the body to repair and regenerate. The effects of relaxation extend far beyond the immediate sense of relief it provides.

Scientific research highlights several benefits of relaxation that go beyond just reducing stress. For example, a 2018 study in Psychoneuroendocrinology found that relaxation techniques, such as mindfulness meditation and deep breathing exercises, can significantly lower cortisol levels, the body's primary stress hormone. In turn, this can lower blood pressure and reduce the risk of cardiovascular disease (Khoury et al., 2018).

Moreover, relaxation has been shown to improve brain function. According to a study published in Psychological

Science, people who practiced mindfulness and relaxation techniques demonstrated improved cognitive performance, including enhanced memory, focus, and decision-making (Zeidan et al., 2010). This highlights that relaxation doesn't only improve mental clarity—it actually helps sharpen your cognitive abilities, giving you the energy and focus you need to be more productive.

2. Creating a Daily Relaxation Ritual

One of the most effective ways to integrate relaxation into your life is by creating a daily ritual. A ritual is more than just a habit; it is a routine that has significance and intention behind it. For example, you might begin each morning with five minutes of deep breathing or finish your day with a meditation session.

The key to successful habit formation lies in consistency. Research conducted by Dr. Phillippa Lally, a health psychologist at the University College London, revealed that it takes on average 66 days for a new behavior to become automatic—longer than many of us expect (Lally et al., 2010). But once a relaxation ritual becomes ingrained in your daily routine, the benefits multiply.

3. Overcoming Barriers to Relaxation

In a world that values constant activity, finding time to relax can feel impossible. Many people cite "lack of time" or "too many responsibilities" as major barriers to incorporating relaxation practices. However, overcoming these barriers is entirely possible when we shift our mindset.

Take Sarah, a working mother of two who once struggled to find time to relax. She used to wake up early, rush through her day, and then collapse into bed at night, feeling mentally exhausted. But after learning about the power of relaxation and its effect on productivity, she committed to setting aside just ten minutes every morning for deep breathing and mindfulness. Slowly, Sarah began to feel the difference—her mind felt clearer, her stress levels lowered, and she even found herself becoming more efficient at work.

The key takeaway? Small, consistent moments of relaxation, even if brief, can have a significant impact on your well-being.

4. Digital Minimalism and the Importance of Downtime

One of the emerging trends in relaxation is the concept of digital minimalism. With the rise of smartphones and constant connectivity, many people find themselves constantly "on," even during their supposed downtime. Taking steps to reduce screen time—especially on social media—can drastically improve your ability to relax and recharge.

Cal Newport, author of Digital Minimalism: Choosing a Focused Life in a Noisy World, argues that minimizing digital distractions allows individuals to engage in deeper forms of relaxation and personal growth. Newport's research suggests that digital minimalism not only improves relaxation but also enhances long-term happiness by giving people the space to engage in more meaningful activities and relationships.

One real-life example comes from John, a corporate executive who felt overwhelmed by the constant buzz of emails and messages. By consciously reducing his screen time after 7 PM, John created a digital-free zone in the evenings. He spent this time reading, journaling, and spending quality time with his family—activities that contributed to his overall relaxation and well-being. His work performance improved, and his relationships became more meaningful as he gave them his undivided attention.

5. How Relaxation Transforms Your Relationships and Productivity

One of the most profound, often overlooked effects of relaxation is its impact on our relationships. When we are relaxed, we are more patient, empathetic, and present with others. The ability to unwind and clear mental clutter fosters emotional resilience, allowing us to better manage conflict and navigate challenging conversations.

In a 2017 study published in the Journal of Applied Psychology, researchers found that relaxation techniques helped individuals in high-stress jobs improve their interpersonal skills and teamwork. The study suggested that employees who practiced relaxation were more likely to experience positive interactions with their coworkers and supervisors (Kabat-Zinn et al., 2017).

Furthermore, relaxation enhances productivity. A well-rested mind is more creative, focused, and effective at solving problems. By integrating moments of relaxation throughout your day, you can boost your overall output, reduce errors, and maintain high levels of energy.

Conclusion: Your Path to a Calm, Clear, and Centered Life

Relaxation is not a luxury—it's a necessity. Whether it's reducing stress, enhancing cognitive function, or fostering deeper connections with others, relaxation is the foundation of a balanced and fulfilling life. As we've seen through real-life examples, scientific research, and emerging trends like digital minimalism, the act of incorporating relaxation into your routine can have a profound impact on your health, relationships, and overall well-being.

To truly benefit from relaxation, start by making it a priority. Design a personalized relaxation ritual, create boundaries around your digital devices, and carve out time for yourself to unwind. Even small, consistent steps can help you achieve lifelong benefits.

The journey toward relaxation doesn't need to be complicated. By making small, mindful changes, you can unlock the power of relaxation, transforming your life in ways you may never have imagined.

Actionable Takeaways

- Create a Daily Relaxation Ritual: Begin with just five to ten minutes of deep breathing, meditation, or journaling each day. Gradually increase this time as it becomes a natural part of your routine.

- Digital Minimalism: Commit to reducing screen time after a certain hour each day to foster a digital-free zone for relaxation.

- Use Relaxation for Relationship Building: Use the calm state achieved through relaxation to improve interactions with loved ones and coworkers. The more present and relaxed you are, the more positive your relationships will be.

Citations

1. Khoury, B., Lecomte, T., Fortin, G., et al. (2018). "Mindfulness-based therapy: A comprehensive meta-analysis." Psychoneuroendocrinology.

2. Zeidan, F., Johnson, S. K., Diamond, B. J., & David, Z. (2010). "Mindfulness meditation

improves cognition: Evidence of brief mental training." Psychological Science.

3. Lally, P., van Jaarsveld, C. H. M., Potts, H. W. W., & Wardle, J. (2010). "How are habits formed: Modelling habit formation in the real world." European Journal of Social Psychology.

4. Kabat-Zinn, J., et al. (2017). "The effects of mindfulness-based stress reduction on perceived stress and well-being in employees." Journal of Applied Psychology.

—◦✦◦—

REFERENCES AND RESOURCES

B elow is a curated list of references and resources to support the content of the chapters in *The Mastery of Relaxation Techniques*. These materials include scientific studies, books, and tools that readers can explore for further learning.

Resources for Further Reading

1. Benson, H., & Proctor, W. (2011). *Relaxation Revolution: The Science and Genetics of Mind Body Healing*. Scribner.

2. McEwen, B. S. (2007). *The End of Stress as We Know It*. Oxford University Press.

3. Newport, C. (2019). *Digital Minimalism: Choosing*

a Focused Life in a Noisy World. Penguin.

4. Tang, Y. Y., Ma, Y., Wang, J., Fan, Y., Feng, S., Lu, Q., & Posner, M. I. (2007). *Short-term meditation training improves attention and self-regulation.* Proceedings of the National Academy of Sciences.

5. Microsoft Research (2021). *The Work Trend Index: The Next Great Disruption Is Hybrid Work.*

Chapter 1: Understanding Stress and Its Impact on Your Well-being

1. Benson, H., & Proctor, W. (2011). *Relaxation Revolution: The Science and Genetics of Mind Body Healing*. Scribner.

2. McEwen, B. S. (2007). *The End of Stress as We Know It*. Oxford University Press.

3. Tang, Y. Y., Ma, Y., Wang, J., Fan, Y., Feng, S., Lu, Q., & Posner, M. I. (2007). *Short-term meditation training improves attention and self-regulation.* Proceedings of the National Academy of Sciences.

4. Microsoft Research (2021). *The Work Trend Index:*

The Next Great Disruption Is Hybrid Work.

Chapter 2: The Art of Deep Breathing for Instant Calm

1. Pascoe, M. C., & Bauer, I. E. (2015). "A Systematic Review of Yoga on Stress Reduction and Mood Enhancement."

2. Smith, C., Hancock, H., Blake-Mortimer, J., & Eckert, K. (2017). "A Randomized Controlled Trial of Yoga for Stress and Anxiety Reduction."

3. Wayne, P. M., et al. (2014). The Harvard Medical School Guide to Tai Chi: 12 Weeks to a Healthy Body, Strong Heart, and Sharp Mind.

4. Sharma, M., & Haider, T. (2018). "The Effects of Stretching on Stress Relief: A Clinical Perspective."

5. Kabat-Zinn, J. (2018). Mindfulness for Beginners: Reclaiming the Present Moment—and Your Life.

Chapter 3: Mastering Mindfulness and Meditation for Lasting Peace

1. Kabat-Zinn, J. (1990). *Full Catastrophe Living: Using the Wisdom of Your Body and Mind to Face Stress, Pain, and Illness.*

2. Goleman, D. (2013). *Emotional Intelligence: Why It Can Matter More Than IQ.*

3. Lazar, S. W., et al. (2005). "Meditation Experience is Associated with Increased Cortical Thickness." *NeuroReport.*

4. Hutcherson, C. A., et al. (2008). "Loving-Kindness Meditation Increases Social Connectedness." *Stanford University Study.*

5. Oman, D., et al. (2008). "Meditation and Health Benefits: A Meta-Analysis." *JAMA Internal Medicine.*

6. Kwekkeboom, K. L. (2003). "Guided Imagery for Managing Pain." *Journal of Behavioral Medicine.*

7. Carlson, L. E., & Garland, S. N. (2005). "Impact of

Mindfulness-Based Interventions on Symptoms of Anxiety and Depression." *Psychosomatic Medicine.*

Chapter 4: Unlocking the Power of Progressive Muscle Relaxation (PMR)

1. Jacobson, E. (1938). *Progressive Relaxation.* University of Chicago Press.

2. Bernstein, D. A., & Borkovec, T. D. (1973). *Progressive Relaxation Training: A Guide for Therapists and Patients.*

3. Conrad, A., & Roth, W. T. (2007). "Muscle relaxation therapy for anxiety disorders: It works but how?" *Journal of Anxiety Disorders.*

4. Mellman, T. A., et al. (1995). "Physiologic alterations associated with sleep deprivation in PTSD." *Journal of Traumatic Stress.*

Chapter 5: The Art of Relaxation—Transforming Stress into Serenity

1. Chanda, M. L., & Levitin, D. J. (2017). "The

neurochemistry of music." *Frontiers in Psychology*.

2. Gao, X., et al. (2014). "Binaural beat effects on brain oscillations and energy expenditure." *Neuroscience Letters*.

3. Hansen, M. M., et al. (2019). "Therapeutic effects of nature soundscapes." *Environmental Health and Preventive Medicine*.

4. Lopez, S. D., et al. (2017). "Neural correlates of nature exposure and relaxation." *Scientific Reports*.

5. Yamamoto, T., & Shinagawa, M. (2018). "Effects of 528 Hz sound on stress reduction." *The Journal of Alternative and Complementary Medicine*.

6. Kabat-Zinn, J. (2013). *Full Catastrophe Living: Using the Wisdom of Your Body and Mind to Face Stress, Pain, and Illness*.

7. Goleman, D. (2003). *Destructive Emotions: A Scientific Dialogue with the Dalai Lama*.

8. Sacks, O. (2007). *Musicophilia: Tales of Music and the Brain*.

9. Bunt, L., & Pavlicevic, M. (2001). *Music and Medicine: The Art and Science of Healing.*

10. Patel, A. D. (2010). *Music, Language, and the Brain.*

Chapter 6: Movement-Based Relaxation: Yoga, Tai Chi, and Stretching

1. The Relaxation and Stress Reduction Workbook by Martha Davis, Elizabeth Robbins Eshelman, and Matthew McKay.

2. Digital Minimalism by Cal Newport.

3. The Miracle of Mindfulness by Thich Nhat Hanh.

4. Wherever You Go, There You Are by Jon Kabat-Zinn.

5. The Art of Rest by Claudia Hammond.

6. Mindfulness in Plain English by Bhante Henepola Gunaratana.

7. The Power of Now by Eckhart Tolle.

These resources provide a robust foundation for deeper understanding and practical application of stress relief strategies covered in *The Mastery of Relaxation Techniques*.

MAY I ASK YOU FOR A SMALL FAVOR?

I want to express my sincere gratitude for choosing to invest your time in reading this book. Your decision to explore this work among countless others means a lot to me.

I hope that within these pages, you've discovered actionable insights that can enhance your daily life. Your journey doesn't have to end here, though.

May I kindly request an additional 30 seconds of your valuable time?

Sharing your thoughts about the book through a review would be immensely appreciated. Your review serves as a beacon, guiding other readers to take a chance on my books. It's a small gesture that carries significant weight in the world of authors.

To submit your review effortlessly, please click on the link below. It will take you directly to the book's review page:

"The Mastery of Relaxation Techniques"

Alternatively, you can also find the "**Reviews Section**" of this book's page on Amazon.

Your review will require just a minute of your time but will make a monumental difference in helping me connect with a broader audience and I eagerly look forward to reading your review.

Once again, thank you for your unwavering support of my work.

—⊰✦⊱—

DISCLAIMER

This book is for educational purposes only. Readers acknowledge that the author does not render legal, financial, medical, or professional advice. The content within this book has been derived from various sources. Please consult a licensed professional before attempting any techniques outlined in this book.

By reading this document, the reader agrees that under no circumstances is the author responsible for any direct or indirect losses incurred as a result of the use of the information contained within this document, including but not limited to errors, omissions, or inaccuracies.

Adherence to all applicable laws and regulations, including international, federal, state, and local governing professional licensing, business practices, advertising, and all other jurisdictions, is the sole responsibility of the purchaser or reader.

Neither the author nor the publisher assumes any responsibility or liability whatsoever on behalf of the purchaser or reader of these materials. Any perceived slight of any individual or organization is purely unintentional.

—◦⊰✦⊱◦—

Printed in Dunstable, United Kingdom